Moments in a Lifetime

Short Poems

JULIE MOTA

jdt
Publications

Text copyright © Julie Mota

Cover illustration copyright © Julie Mota

First Edition: July, 2018

The moral right of the author has been asserted.

Published by JDT Publications
Port Moresby, NCD, Papua New Guinea
Email: jdtpublications@gmail.com

National Library of Papua New Guinea
Cataloguing-in-Publication entry:

Mota, Julie. 1978 — .
    Moments in a Lifetime: Short Poems.
    p. ; cm.

ISBN-13: 978-9980-901-78-1

1. Poetry, Papua New Guinea.
i. JDT Publications.   ii. Title.
PNG/821/M67/M65– dc22

Printed in USA by CreateSpace Independent Publishing.

For Rachel Betty Mota and Marian Leboh Koi Kondi
who challenged my perceptions of the world through their lives.

I want to thank God Almighty for this opportunity to publish this book.

There are so many people I want to thank in getting this collection published and I thank each and every one of you.

To Jordan Dean, a writer with a heart for the development of contemporary Papua New Guinean literature. Thank you so much for your generosity, encouragements and support in my work.

To Keith Jackson, Phil Fitzpatrick and Michael Dom for the review of my first poetry collection *'Cultural Refugees'* on PNG Attitude and all the people who have encouraged me to publish my poems via Poetry PNG group on Facebook.

To my family who have supported my creative endeavors, glory be to God. To Bernard, Anne-Lyn, Andrew and Marian, thank you so much for being a part of my life.

To Terry Tangole and family, Susan Govaik and our Ruango Sculpture Garden friends, thank you for your friendship that has helped me through the writing period.

To Dr. Uluk and Dr. Longa-Irisa and their staff of Children's Clinic and ward at Kimbe Provincial Hospital who have for the past two and a half years shared my pain and struggle to understand my daughter's medical condition. Christian friends and families around the world especially our Catholic community here at Kimbe Catholic Diocese for the friendship and fellowship through the tough times. May God bless you all.

Through the tears and emotional turmoil I have found my voice through poetry.

CONTENTS

PREFACE

This is a collection of poems about a personal journey that has been an interesting and exciting one, exploring the daily lifestyle situations of people in Papua New Guinea. It explores the different situations and life stages and initiates a discussion on the values of life and family as an important institution on human relationships.

Has life changed much in the past few years since independence? How has the different aspects of traditional lifestyle changed and to what extent can we say that urbanization has had an impact on our local, indigenous cultural practices and its human relationships? In the same instance, when social spaces are displaced, physical spaces tend to lose their cultural significance and in turn affects the social connections and networking.

After all, communal heritage spaces for cultural consumption are an integral aspect of indigenous communities and the rapid transitional phase of traditional way of life to the modern cash community has been a contributing factor to the continual cultural erosion of oral histories and the destruction of cultural heritage sites. This in turn has affected social relationships of people with regard to maintaining kinship relationships and obligations.

This collection *'Moments in a Lifetime'* is an appreciation of the old way of story-telling or passing important anecdotes of life through the use of figurative impressions of nature. In my culture, important lessons about life are taught through the study of the natural

9

environment. It is a collection of my journey in life through interpretations with nature.

This is my second anthology of poems. *'Cultural Refugees'* was published early this year.

I hope that you will enjoy reading this collection.

Julie Mota
July, 2018

MORNING BREEZE

Early morning breeze
In lithe brief gentle touch
Caress me again.

EVENING

The day ends
Curtains of day roll on
Another chapter closes.

GOOD DAY

Calm oceans views
In the clear blue sky
Graciously greet me.

HEAVENLY TEARS

Heavenly tears fall
Washing away all the dust
Rejuvenation at last.

RARE PEOPLE

Diamonds are rare
Teaches us all a lesson too
Godly people are rare.

MY SECRET

And nobody knows
Too very deep all in me.
Life's sweet misery.

RESTING

All asleep now
Not a wink or stir
Rest is sweet.

SELF-PITY

Drown in sorrow
Deep hurts that stings bite
fleeting hopes dashed.

PAINFUL MEMORIES

Moon hung low
Dim glow of memories shone
Flashing hurts anew.

WISHES

Full moon shines
My heart soars high above
Sweet dreams tonight.

BUSY HANDS

A mother's love
Season's tale too harsh hush
Her busy hands.

WET SEASON

Wet season arrives
Soggy tears bursting through again
Wailing child indeed.

BATTERED BLUE

Battered blue and wasted through
Lovers games that are gone sorely awry
It's domestic violence lame excuse.

SUNSET ABBOT

Like an abbot on a mission
The last rays follow the lone fisherman
Paddling out to the sea.

LONGING

When the moon is high
Stars are bright up in the sky
I long for your company.

MUSING

Swift through all the hurt
The bitterness lie buried deep and neat
A lesson or two abides.

GUILT

Hate, brute, unsaid, undefined, deeds
No one should know the lies that sears
Better tests of one's hearts.

LIFE SCENES

Hum drum of life
Fleeting scenes passing
With twists and turns.

DAY'S END

Curtains of the day sway
In gentle teasing waves
Another day ends.

DISTANCE LOVE

If I could touch you
Minus the distance and time with it
Bitter sweet honey taste desserts.

REJUVENATION

The first streaks of light
In the sky of solemn truths lie
Lives anew are rejuvenated.

SEASONED WORDS

Seasoned words in time echoes
In my mind flavors of words whisper
Rhyming words that ring true.

JEALOUS

Raving madness and seething hatred
Courting lies and playing fires letting fly
Riding on a moments spur.

WAN MINIT BIKSOT

San ino go daun yet
Moni kapsait yet oksem wara
Tank buruk na yumi lukim.

POET

Poets are actors mincing words
Like feathers soaring high in rhythm tunes
The post scripts in blue sky rings.

Little tassels of sweet hopes
Humanity dews of sweet hopes soar high
In due verses beat away.

Tempos and melodies sing anyway
Poets and actors all that mince words
Sing them tunes humming too.

DAMS OF HEAVEN

Heaven's dam burst open wide
The soil sucked it all up.

Little blessings on our path
Small players all the same.

Daily offerings to our needs
We only need to ask.

EVENING DESCENDS

Silver linings on the last rays
As a fisherman paddles out.

The rush hour drizzles
A smooth ride home.

Evening shades descends
Weariness starts sweeping.

It has been a long day
As time gently rushes by.

People with memories
Don't say goodbye.

Julie Mota

Painful Truths

Like first streaks of light
Little lives bloom in view.

Unearth buried truths lie too
Solemn hurts awake and sting.

Poets are Actors too

Mincing words to a tune
Postscript in blue to lure.

Tassels of hope sweet dew
Show us hues of humanity.

In due verse of beat and tempo
Poets melodies ring with beat too.

DESIRE

Blooming red today burning hot
Passionate tales, secrets and lies.

It's never too late song is sung.
But it's broken heart so far away.

CHEAP GRIN

Cheap grin plastic doll
Wasted wares all same.

Empty lives no goals
Shallow minded little lives.

HARVEST RUN

Faithful servant abide now
Wait patiently now for dole.

Oh the mill runs now
They still run the mills.

 I complain so much
So late and depressing.

God hear deliver me now
Heavens gates open wide.

MIXED EMOTIONS

Reminder of things best forgotten
Like prophet of doom hauntings.

The little pleasures of life sprout
Living for time and life ride together.

Vanished banished into our past too
Date with destiny not fantasy alone.

You were real and we were thrilled
So surreal but to reveal will defeat me.

DARK LIES

When fear instills such hatred
Deep coals of distrusts sears.

Community panics by such folly
Shame and understanding gone.

Christianity too loses its grip
Heinous crimes are committed

When human fear fuels again
Another lie a life is gone soon.

Sorcery related violence is real
It has to stop and soon too.

GRADUATION

Sun's scorching heat
Burning flame in my heart
Dusty days of strive and frays
Will all disappear.

Promises renewed
Tomorrows hopes seems near
Sweat and grit shall cease
To a new tune I hear.

GURIA

In a flash moments too fast
In an instant took my breath away.

To sing and swaying like a rag doll
Head spinning legs wobbly drowning.

In a waving motion surfing around
A rag doll out of control so unpleasant.

FEAR

Deaths dark gloom and doom
In evening dim light
Shadows moving along
CREEPY
CRAWLY
CLAWS reach out
S C R E A M!

RONOWE

Papa dok
Mama dok
Pikinini dok
Bung lo rot.

Painim wok
Wokim wok
Na em wok.

Wok blo tok
Na mi todok
Displa todok.

LITTLE LIES

Little lies to big lies
To his wife such is his life
Of lies so his wife dies
As his lies so he lives and dies
LIAR!

LOVE AND LUST

Love is labors
Lust is a sloth
Love is patient
Lust is burns fiercely.

Love is kind
Lust is a conqueror
Love is long suffering
Lust demands attention.

Love is tolerant
Lust is self-conceited
Love unites
Lust divides
Love adds
Lust subtracts
Better wise now.

MARIT BURUK

Pen em stap laip em go
Tumoro stap aste go
Nao em nao laip em olsem tasol.

Tingim stap planti pen
Hat long lus tinting pen blo graun
Hat long toktok.

SAMTIN BLO SKELIM

San igat kik win gat nem
Ren gat sign man na meri yumi mas skelim gut
Tok pilai gat mak banis blo laip tu noken paol
Nogut yu lus noken driman opim ai na stap
Hevi stap lon doa noken opim doa natnating
Skelim tok na trautim yu yet nao.

FALSE PIETY

Holy month with false piety appears
Dress and doll for all to see
Dabbing lies on her tongue
Deceitful game plans on the move
Same pretense wolves in deer skins
No saint just rain pain faint domain
No shame blasphemy to our faith
Leading hate with her mate all along
Shades, fades, raises, divides, debates
I rest my case.

DOMESTIC VIOLENCE

Silent tears, deep anguish, troubled thoughts
Unsettled minds in weariness they tarry
For sullen lies with screaming threats
pounding charges into the night of terror
In between the punches and the kicks
Flashes of blows inflicting deep wounds
Of broken dreams and shedding hopes
For tomorrow's innocent children lovers no more
Defeated amongst the reverberating turns
All too fast, too soon a family's pain.

SOUL MATES

My best friend forever together
In good times and bad times
Through seasons of time
We walk the earth together
The blues and the tunes
Crazy lovers remain true
My child, my hope.

Tomorrow awaits you at dawn
Yesterday's promises to guide you
Our family's dreams and hopes
Are in your hands now.

BIRTHRIGHT

In birth by blood relation
In kinship ties our identity
Establishes our property rights
Our status in community
My son.

My strength
My joy
My future
Fruit of my womb
My son.

BLEST

I shall not complain nor nag neither sigh
I'm alive, I eat, sleep, I live, love feel, taste
Life is a bitter sweet tale of misfits
Oh, thorns and weeds cursed be cast you
Rebuke, retreat I go in life.

DEEP SORROW

What sorrow so deep
Breath so in life
Bitter sweet love
'Till we meet.

GORGOR BLO PLES

Saitim tok pisin tumas
Olsem ol kotkot blo bus
Olgeta tok blo tok pinis
Pilis gorgor blo ples tumas.

POETS NOTES

Poets rambling case book
Noting little life's pleasures
Weaving all dancing words
Together as one in tunes
A season's green.

Greenery moods bloom like nature
Carpets of green cover earth
Merry emotions ring through
Giving, living a season's green.

SHELL RIDE ART

Destiny's date
Reusing old ideas
Installations art
A wreck or art decor.

KUSAI TASOL

Na sapos ibin stret em bai hau?
Mangi Sandaun lusim olsem tasol
San go daun nao lon solwara
Larim nao yumi lusim olsem tasol.

HOPE

In pitch darkness a light lights up
Moonlights are not yet up
It is only you and I
But tomorrow is a moment away.

FLIRTATIONS

A gifted hand
Brilliant mind
Yet a lonely soul
Once drifted this way
Where a beautiful heliconia bloomed.

On the myriad side
With its bewitching charmed seduced him
Full of fragrance such beauty and zest for life
He reached out to claim it but it remained rooted.

Bathing in the sun bewitching temptress
So he left defeated and shunned
Because for every garden there's a gardener.

MOON LIGHT ILLUSIONS

Light so bright
Up so high looking down
Peals of laughter ring in the corridors
Choir has ended let the young people laugh.

Stars that brighten up the sky oh so long
Silhouettes on the beach where waves splash
Breaking on the shores and romantic illusions play
Little hearts alight hopes soar high.

BROKEN

Mountains and valleys
Rivers and forests
Hamlets and valleys
Moments in time.

City life too high awhile away
In eyes of pride racing in time
Speeding past too fast
Belittling all of us too
Demands too high
Pressing us down.

Sweet bitter life murmurs
A nation's dreams in our lives
A moment in a life time.

DEPRESSED

When the road is long and seems no end
Hope is fading to a stop
Joy has gone
Laughter disappears and silence reigns.

Life is not fair sometimes
And depressingly true
Yet hopes beacon shall shine once again
To fade away the worries that sail
And we will sing victory blues again.

A TIRING DAY

Been long hard day toiling the work too hard.
Now the body gives in to rest
Sleepy eyes close up for the night.

CURSE OF JEALOUSY

Such trickery of wounded words that come to hurt
With lies from evil intents to pain
Dragon fly in wanton spur
Spit venomous hate in an empty heart
Mockery's little dance knocking
At the door of a feeble mind.

LADY OF THE NIGHT

The lady of the night bloomed tonight
And we danced the slow waltz
Of light prune
Nips at the edge
Trimmed and set
Neat beauty in my view.

MI NO SAVE WAI?

Bipo marit blo sidaonim femli
Nau planti marit buruk tumas
Bikpla hevi blo sidaun
Pikinini tu lusim save blo femli.

WOUNDED SOUL

By the brook it laid
A broken will of a fallen restless soul
Blinkers and all
Haughty pride and smitten lies
Slothful gluttony finding its way to repentance
All the while it laid.

A NIGHTMARE

Fireflies glow in the dark corners only
Like little reminders
Crickets high pitch light up the dark corners
In sound effects
The gentle breeze waltz by in quiet confidence
The show begins
Creatures queer appear perhaps only in my dreams
They stare at me
Darkness sings aloud an eerie tale of fear
Time to steer
With dawn afar terror reeks in the air
Panic is appearing nightly flights abound
Running in the darkness blind
Alert, awake and away
Gasps and cries as sweat builds into rivers
A fever pitch level torment my sanity
I scream
But it's just a dream.

LIFE OF A VILLAGER

A soft and light touch
Cleanse and soothes my breath
It greets me on the way up
Twigs crackle, leaves rustle and wave
Birds fly above as the forest floor greet us
Color palette dazzle under the sun light
Earth welcomes the new day
The forest welcomes the farmer
Life moves on for a villager
In our part of the world.

ABOUT THE AUTHOR

Julie Mota a freelance artist and writer based in Kimbe, West New Britain Province, Papua New Guinea. She is married and has three children.

She has been involved in Creative Arts for almost two decades producing, exhibiting and teaching art through community development projects. She has travelled to some the most remote places where she was challenged by the daily struggles of ordinary Papua New Guineans.

The encounters are a constant reminder for her to value life. Julie seeks to understand those challenges through her poetry.